AN INTRODUCTION TO COMPUTERS

Volume Two

Nwaiwu Ifeanyi Princewill

ISBN
978-1-4828-8083-0 (sc)
978-1-4828-8084-7 (e)

Print information available on the last page.

To order additional copies of this book, contact
Toll Free 800 101 2657 (Singapore)
Toll Free 1 800 81 7340 (Malaysia)
www.partridgepublishing.com/singapore
orders.singapore@partridgepublishing.com

01/11/2017

PARTRIDGE

SKCBT Computer Series

Smart Kids Computer Brain Tutor Literacy Program 21st Century Series

Second Edition 2015

Classification: Course Learning / Activity Learning

Published and distributed by SKCBT Store, Corp. (SKCBT with main office at House No. 321A, Street 41BT Bouing Tom Pou, Meanchey, Phnom Penh, Cambodia;

Tel: (+855) 97-992-2810 / (+855) 11-469-061;

E-mail: customercare@skcbt.com or info@skcbt.com

Website: www.skcbt.com

Regional Office: No. 15B Oparanozie Street Owerri, Imo State, Nigeria;

Tel: (+234) 7037129291 / (+234) 8022873751;

E-mail: princecomputerbooks@yahoo.com or princecomputerbooks@gmail.com

Website: www.skcbt.com

i

Certificate

This is to endorse that this Book titled SmartKids Computer Brain Tutor personified the original work done by Engr. **Nwaiwu Princewill Ifeanyi**.

Editors: **Ms. Emily Mackay
(Canada)**

**Ms. Wirsiy Stella
(Cameroun)**

ACKNOWLEDGEMENTS

This book is the reflection of many illuminating and liberating learning concepts that have affected our lives.

I am indebted to Mr. Nwaiwu Stephen, Dr. Humphrey Amadi (Lecturer AICE), Engr. Huy (Lecturer NIIT Cambodia) and Mr. Clifford Michael (Lecturer Limkokwing University Cambodia) whose training and legacy has affected me in the most tremendous way and God Almighty who made it possible for me.

TEACHING GUIDE

EDUCATIONAL OBJECTIVES

Cognitive, Affective and Psychomotor domain

(The Role of a Teacher in 21st Century)

- **Individualist Learning** (The Teacher provides the major source of information, assistance, criticism and feedback; students work alone and not expected to be interrupted by other students)

- **Co-operative Learning** (Students work together in small clusters or groups)

- **Collaborative Learning** (This takes place when students cooperate to construct a consensus to an open-ended activity e.g students interacting with each other for a solution)

- **Competitive Learning** (When one student's goal is achieved, all other students will fail to reach that goal and it becomes a motivator for others)

AIM

The aim of this book module is to help 1st – 6th grade students with little or no computer experience understand the basics of how computers work and how to use them.

RATIONALE

Technology is an integral part of daily life and students need equal and adequate access to it. The use of technology as a learning tool can make a measurable difference in student's achievement, attitudes, and interactions with teachers and other students. Students are more challenged, more engaged, and more independent.

PRE-REQUISITES

Basic reading skills

SUBJECT-MATTER

Basic computer terms like disk, origin of computer and functions of the keys of the Keyboard, etc.

GOALS & OBJECTIVES

Students will:

1. Differentiate between different types of storage devices
2. Demonstrate correct use of input and output devices to operate a computer
3. Show knowledge of what the origin of computer means
4. Use a search engine
5. Navigate on the Internet

INSTRUCTIONAL PLAN

This book module is designed to be used as part of a teachers directed lessons in a computer lab. Following the lessons presented to the entire class in the lab, students will be able to complete the activities individually or in small groups. The activities will provide students with the opportunity to develop and reinforce the skills presented during the lessons. Although studentswillcomplete the activities at different pacesdepending on their level, the teacher should set a reasonable time limit.

MATERIALS

1. Desktop Computer with Internet access

2. Appropriate software

3. Printer

4. Pencil

5. Eraser

6. Sharpener

7. Colour Pencils

ASSESSMENT & EVALUATION

Assessment includes:

1. Teacher observation

2. Workbook (Quick Check)

3. Summary of each chapter(s)

INTRODUCTION TO COMPUTER - 2 (Explorer)

Contents

INTRODUCTION TO COMPUTER - 2 (Explorer)

COMPUTER

Lesson – 1.1: Definition of computer

Definition of a Computer

- A Computer is an electronic device that <u>input</u>, <u>process</u>, <u>output</u> and <u>stores data</u>.

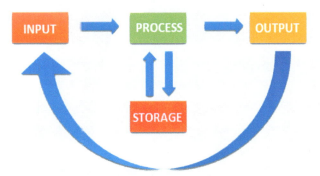

The word "computer" was first recorded as being used in 1613 and was originally used to describe a person who performed calculations or computations. The definition of a computer remained the same until the end of the 19th century when it began referring to a machine that performed calculations.

- **<u>INPUT</u>**: Computer accepts data when we type.

- **<u>PROCESS</u>**: Computer checks what we typed on the keyboard.

- **<u>OUTPUT</u>**: Computer displays what we typed on the monitor.

- **<u>STORES DATA</u>**: Computer saves our work on computer memory.

<u>INPUT, PROCESS, OUTPUT & STORES DATA</u>

PARTS OF COMPUTER	FUNCTION(S)	PARTS OF COMPUTER	FUNCTION(S)
Monitor	Output	Mouse	Input
Modem	Process	Microphone	Input
System Unit	Process /Storage	Speaker	Output
Scanner	Input	Printer	Output
Keyboard	Input	Ear-Phone	Output

Lesson – 1.2: BASIC CHARACTERISTICS OF A COMPUTTER?

Part(s)	Function(s)
Mouse and Keyboard  <image of keyboard and mouse>	⊞ Mouse and Keyboard are used to communicate with the computer. ⊞ They are **input** devices.
Speaker and Earphone  <image of speakers and earphone>	⊞ These are **output** devices that allow you to listen to music or sound from the computer.
Scanner and microphone  <image of scanner and microphone>	⊞ A Scanner is used to copy an image into the computer. ⊞ A Microphone is used to capture voice and sound into the computer. ⊞ They are also **input** devices.

System Unit (CPU) 	⊞ The System Unit has a processor which serves as the brain of the computer. It processes data and instructions. ⊞ It also stores data and programs to be used by the CPU. ⊞ It is a **processor** and a **storage device**.
Monitor 	⊞ It displays data that you input and information on the screen. ⊞ It is an **output** device.
Printers 	⊞ All kinds of printers are known as output devices. ⊞ A Printer is used to print our work on a hard-copy.

DOC - (QUICK-CHECK-1)

6

Date: _____

DEFINITION OF COMPUTER

1. Tick the definition of computers.

| Computers are objects that can breathe, talk, display data and walk on two legs. | Computers are devices that have the ability to input, process, output and store data. |

2. Use the given clues to complete the crossword puzzle.

Across
2. The computer displays what we typed on the screen or hardcopy.

Down
1. The computer saves our work on computer memory.
3. The computer checks what we typed on the keyboard.
4. The computer accepts data when we type.

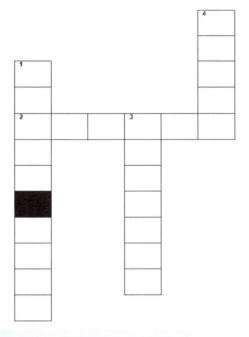

DOC - (QUICK-CHECK-2)

$\overline{6}$

Date: _____

Use the given clues to complete the crossword puzzle below.

Down
1. It is an output device that produces sound.
2. It is an output device that displays information on the screen.
3. It is an input device you use to communicate with the computer by typing.

Across
4. It is a process device and the brain of the computer.
5. It is an output device that produces hard copies.
6. It is an input device you use to point at any part of the screen.

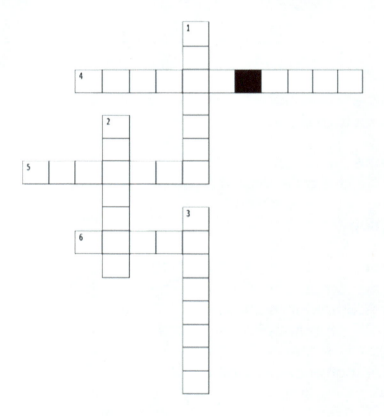

DOC - (QUICK-CHECK-3)

$\overline{3}$

Date: _____

Complete the following representation of the Von-Neumann machine using the following information below:

(Storage,   Output,   Input)

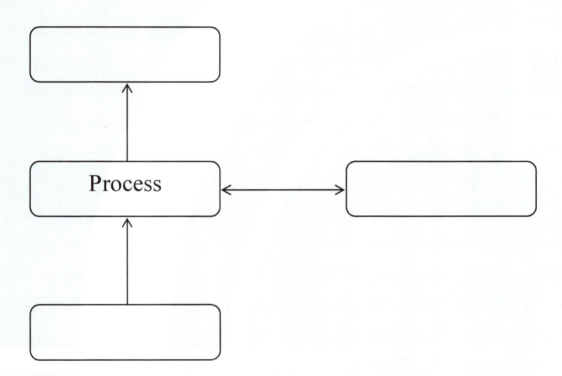

THE DISK

Lesson – 2.1: What is a Disk?

A **disk** is a plate that stores information.

Floppy Disk

Compact Disc

Memory Stick

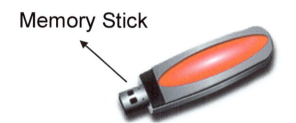

8

The Disk Song

Disk is a plate,
that stores information /,

Disk is a plate,
that stores information \,

Disk is a plate,
that stores information /,

ask me my name,
I will tell you the disk.

Lesson – 2.2: Types of Disks.

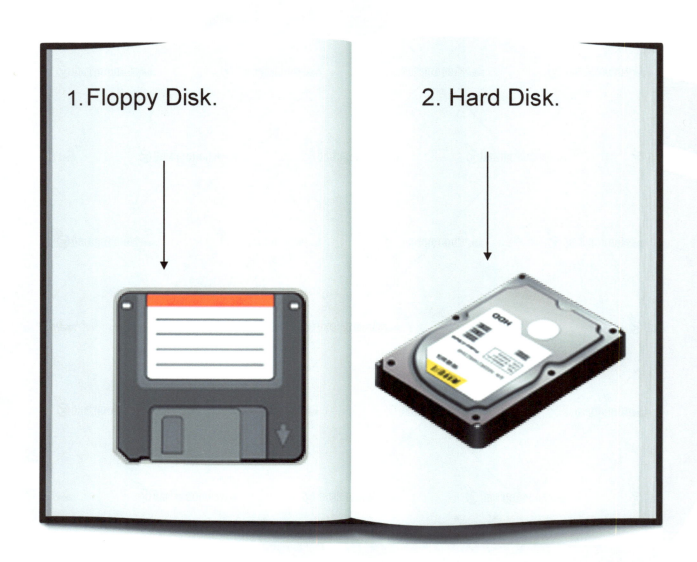

1. Floppy Disk.

2. Hard Disk.

TYPES OF FLOPPY DISKS

A.) 3.5 inches–floppy disk

B.) 5.25 inches–floppy disk

C.) 8 inches–floppy disk

3.5"   5.25"

8"

TYPES OF HARD DISK

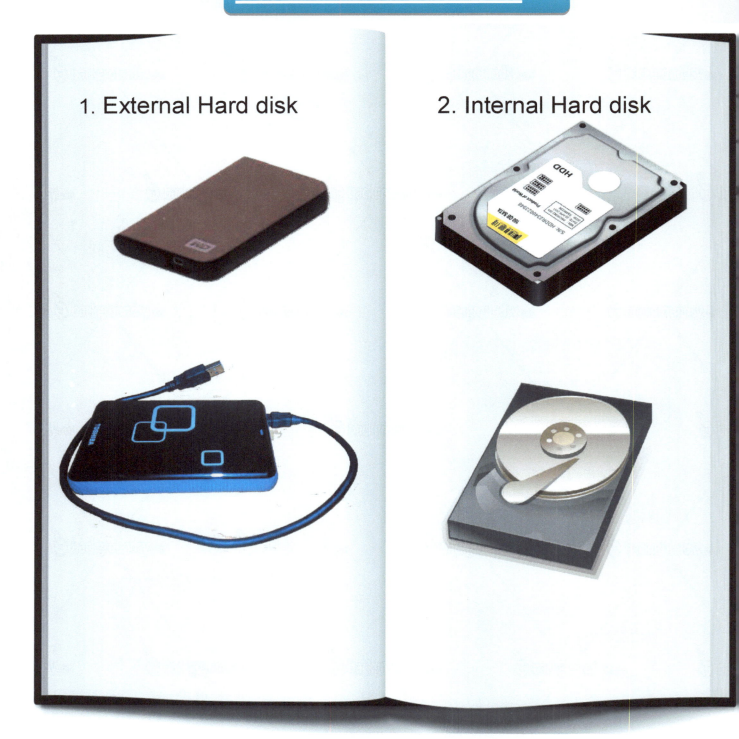

1. External Hard disk

2. Internal Hard disk

INTRODUCTION TO COMPUTER - 2 (Explorer)

Types of Disk Song

One two three,
Oh! one two three,

One two three,
Oh! one two three,

One two three,
Oh! one two three,

Is a floppy and a hard disk.

13

TD - (QUICK-CHECK-1)

$\overline{8}$

Date: _____

Fill in the blank spaces with the appropriate word.

1. **Name three types of floppy disk.**

   i.) _____

   ii.) _____

   iii.) _____

2. **Name two types of hard disk.**

   i.) _____

   ii.) _____

3. **Label the names of the storage devices below.**

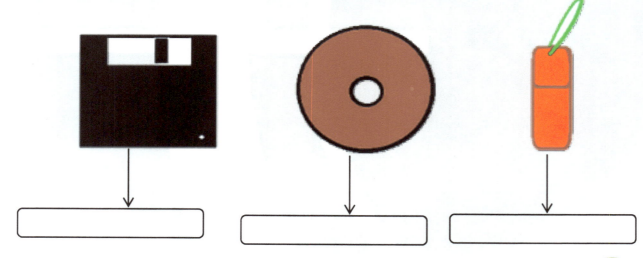

14

TD - (QUICK-CHECK-2)

$$\frac{-}{3}$$

Date: _____

Choose the options in parenthesis to fill-in the blank spaces.

1) What type of device is a 3.5-inch floppy drive?   (   )

a) Input   b) Output   c) Software   d) Storage

2) What type of devices is CDs or DVDs?   (   )

a) Input   b) Output   c) Software   d) Storage

3) What type of device is a digital camera?   (   )

a) Input   b) Output   c) Software   d) Storage

15

Chapter - 3

ORIGIN OF COMPUTER

Lesson – 3.1: What is Origin?

➢ The *Origin* is the point at which something started from.

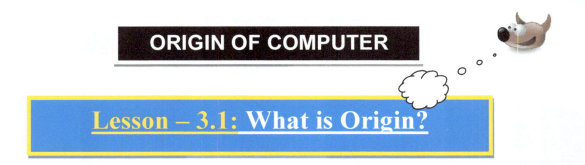

➢ *The Origin* **of a computer** is when we started seeing a computer.

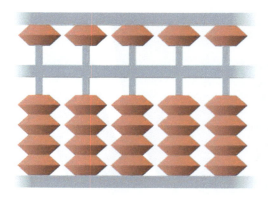

Lesson – 3.2: The First Computer

1.) The first computer was introduced in the year **1941**.

2.) The man that introduced the First Computer is called **Howard Aiken**.

3.) The name given to the First Computer is **Automatic Sequence Controlled Computer (ASCC).**

17

Lesson - 3: The First Electronic Computer.

1.) The First Electronic Computer was introduced in the year **1943**.

2.) The man that introduced the First Electronic Computer is called **John Von Neumann.**

3.) The name given to the First Electronic Computer is the **Electronic Numerical Integrator and Computer (ENIAC).**

Summary

1. **Computer** is an electronic machine that inputs, process, outputs and stores data.

2. **Disk** is a plate that stores information.

3. **Input:** Computer accepts data when we type.

4. **Process:** Computer checks what we type on the keyboard.

5. **Output:** Computer displays what we type on the monitor.

6. **Storage:** Computer saves our work on computer memory.

7. The first computer was introduced in the year **1941**.

8. The man that introduced the First Computer is called **Howard Aiken**.

9. The name given to the First Computer is **Automatic Sequence Controlled Computer (ASCC).**

10. The First Electronic Computer was introduced in the year **1943**.

11. The man that introduced the First Electronic Computer is called **John Von Neumann.**

12. The name given to the First Electronic Computer is **Electronic Numerical Integrator and Computer (ENIAC).**

OOC - (QUICK-CHECK-1)

4

Date: _____

Write the missing word or letters in each statement.

1. Origin of _____ is when we started seeing a computer.

2. The first computer was introduced in the year 19_____.

3. The man that introduced the First Computer is called H_____
   A_____.

4. The name given to the First Computer is Aut_____atic Se_____ence
   Cont_____lled Computer (ASCC).

5. Who is this _____ ?   (   )

   a. John Von Neumann
   b. Howard Aiken
   c. John Kennedy

20

OOC - (QUICK-CHECK-2) | 4 | Date: _____

Write the missing word or letters in each statement.

1. The First Electronic Computer was introduced in the year

    _____.

2. The man that introduced the First Electronic Computer is called J_____

    V_____ N_____.

3. The name given to the First Computer is

    El_____tronic Nu_____rical Int_____rator and Computer (ENIAC).

4. Who is this   ?   (   )

    a. John Von Neumann
    b. John Kennedy
    c. Howard Aiken

Chapter - 4

TAKING CARE OF THE COMPUTER

LESSON – 4.1 : COMPUTER CARING

1.)   Avoid exposing your computer to heat.

2.)   Do not use magnetic objects near the computer.

3.)   Do not move the computer around.

4.)   Do not take food or drink to the computer room.

5.)   Always plug your computer to an **Uninterrupted Power Supply**.

6.) Turn off the computer when a brownout occurs.

7.) Shut down your computer properly.

8.) Take off your shoes before you enter the computer room.

9.)   Shut the door of the computer room properly.

10.)   Always tidy up the computer room.

INTRODUCTION TO COMPUTER - 2 (Explorer)

LESSON – 4.2: HOW TO TURN-ON THE COMPUTER

In order to use a computer, it must be powered-on and this lesson is very important for any Computer Operator to note.

Steps on how to Turn-on the Computer;

1.)   Turn on the switch at the source of the POWER SUPPLY.

2.)   Turn on the UPS to regulate the flow of current.

3.)   Turn on the **POWER SWITCH** of the Monitor.

4.)   Turn on the SYSTEM UNIT.

LESSON – 4.3: HOW TO TURN-OFF THE COMPUTER

It is good to turn off the computer properly to avoid damage or hard start of the computer.

Steps on how to Turn-off the Computer;

1. Click on **Start Button.**

2. Next, click on **shut button**, or **Turn off Computer**.

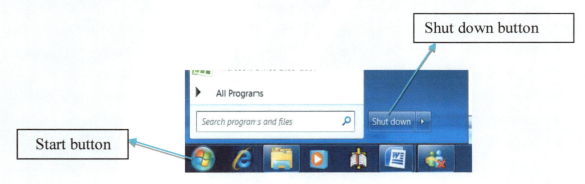

3. Turn off computer dialog-box will display, then
   You click on **Turn off** (Stand By ⊠, Turn off ☑, Restart ⊠)

4. After that you allow the screen to display black background.

5. Then turn-off the power switch of the Monitor.

PC: - means Personal Computer.

UPS: - means Un-Interrupted Power Supply.

LESSON – 4.4: SHUTDOWN BUTTON FUNCTIONS

Types of shutdown buttons:

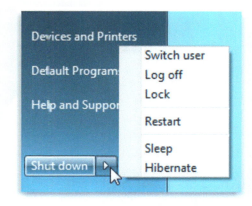

1. Switch User

2. Log Off

3. Lock

4. Restart

5. Sleep/Standby

6. Hibernate

29

1. <u>**Switch User:**</u> It is an easy way for another person to log on to the computer without logging you off or closing your programs and files.

Steps:

i. Click the Start button , and then click the arrow next to the

   Shut Down button .

ii. Click Switch User.

2. <u>**Log Off**</u>: Desktop log-off end all the process you are using in your profile account.

3. <u>**Lock:**</u> Desktop Lock, none can access your documents, browse your computer, or use programs on your computer.

4. <u>**Restart:**</u> it allows you to start up your computer when it fails.

5. <u>**Sleep:**</u> It allows you to set the computer to auto-sleep to save on computer energy use.

6. <u>**Hibernation**</u>: It is shutting down a computer while keeping unsaved files and unclosed programs.

LESSON – 4.5: HOW TO CREATE DESKTOP USER ACCOUNT

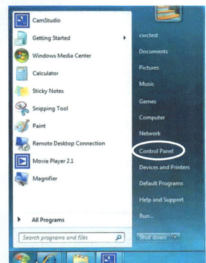

1. Click on **start button**

2. Next, click on **Control Panel**

3. Next, click to **add or remove** user account

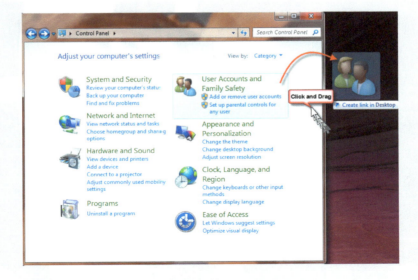

4. Click to **create a new account**

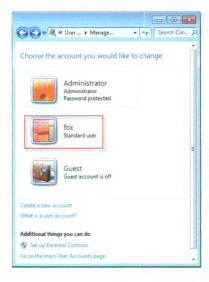

5. Enter your **user name**

Name the account and choose an account type

This name will appear on the Welcome screen and on the Start menu.

YIM DARA

○ Standard user

Standard account users can use most software and change system settings that do not affect other users or the security of the computer.

◉ Administrator

Administrators have complete access to the computer and can make any desired changes. To help make the computer more secure, administrators are asked to provide their password or confirmation before making changes that affect other users.

We recommend that you protect every account with a strong password.

Why is a standard account recommended?

Create Account   Cancel

6. Then click **create account**

Your user account will be automatically created.

LESSON – 4.6: HOW TO PERSONALISE YOUR COMPUTER

⊞ CHANGE YOUR DESKTOP BACKGROUND

Step:

1. Right click on your desktop.
2. Click Personalise

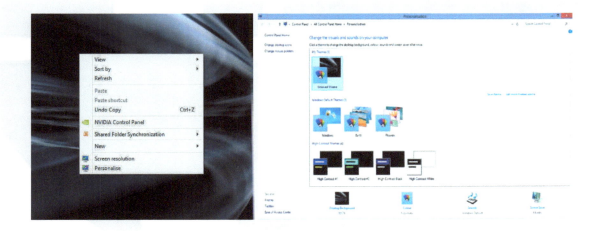

INTRODUCTION TO COMPUTER - 2 (Explorer)

3. Next, click on Desktop Background.

4. Select the background of your choice.
5. Then click Save Change.

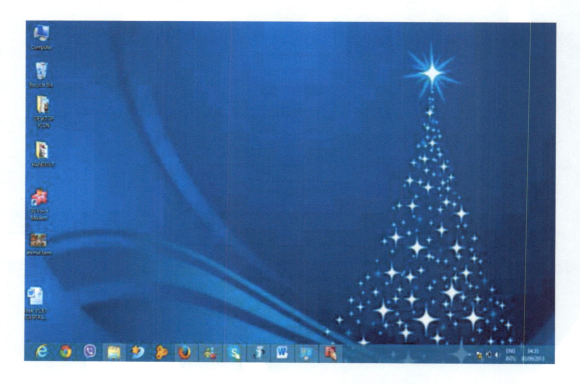

34

⊞ TO CHANGE COLOUR OF YOUR WINDOW BORDERS AND TASKBAR

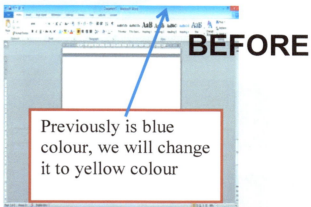

BEFORE

Previously is blue colour, we will change it to yellow colour

Step:

1. Click on Colour.

2. Then click Save Change.

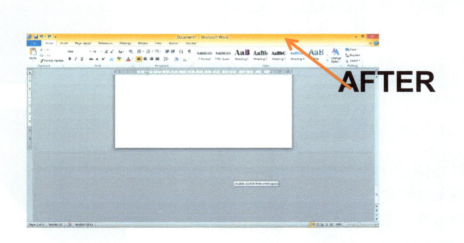

AFTER

35

INTRODUCTION TO COMPUTER - 2 (Explorer)

TO CHANGE SOUND SCHEME

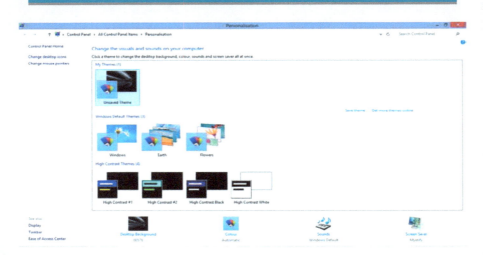

STEP

1. Click the sound.
2. Sound dialog box will display.

3. Next, select window start-up sound and program event sound.
4. Next, click apply.
5. Then click OK.
6. Automatically the sound will apply.

TO SET A SCREENSAVER

1. Click on screensaver
2. Screen saver setting d alog-box will display.

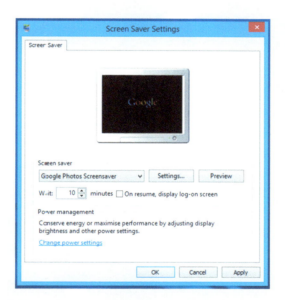

3. Choose the theme of your choice.
4. Next, click apply.
5. Then click OK.

37

⊞ TO SET DESKTOP GADGETS

1. Right click on your desktop screen.
2. Click gadgets.

3. The gadgets dialog-box will display.
4. Double-click type of gadgets you want to display on desktop screen.

5. Automatically your choice of gadgets like clock, calendar etc., will display on the right of the screen.

38

TO SET/CHANGE USER ACCOUNT PICTURE

Steps:

1. Click the Start button , and then click the Control Panel.

2. Control Panel Dialog-box will display.
3. Click on Add or Remove User Accounts.

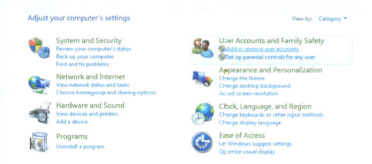

4. Click on User Account you want to change.

5. Click on Change the Picture.

6. Select the picture you want to display on your User Account.

7. Then click Change Picture.
8. Automatically the picture will display or replace the old picture.

9. Click on User Account you want to change.

Summary

1. **UPS** *means* Un-Interrupted Power Supply

2. **PC** *means* Personal Computer.

3. **Log Off:** Desktop log-off end all the process you are using in your profile account.

4. **Lock:** Desktop Lock, none can access your documents, browse your computer, or use programs on your computer.

5. **Restart:** it allows you to start up your computer when it fails.

6. **Sleep:** It allows you to set the computer to auto-sleep to save on computer energy use.

7. **Hibernation:** It is shutting down a computer while keeping unsaved files and unclosed programs.

8. **CP** means Control Panel.

HCC - (QUICK-CHECK-1)

10

Date: _____

Choose the options in parenthesis to fill-in the blank spaces.

> supply,   move,   shut,   heat,   Turn-off, computer,
> door,   room,   shoes,   food,   drink

1. Avoid exposing your computer to _____.

2. Do not use magnetic object near the _____.

3. Do not _____ the computer around.

4. Do not take _____ or _____ to the computer room.

5. Always plug your computer to an Uninterrupted Power _____ (UPS).

6. _____ the computer when a brownout occurs.

7. _____ down your computer properly.

8. Take off your _____ before you enter the computer room.

9. Shut the _____ of the computer room properly.

10. Always tidy up the computer _____.

HCC - (QUICK-CHECK-2)

$\overline{6}$

Date: _____

(Write the answer on the bracket provided)

1. _____ is used to go to another account on the screen.
   ( )
   a. switch user   b. log off   c. lock

2. _____ is used to sign out from an account.   ( )
   a. sleep   b. log off   c. lock

3. _____ is used to rest when one is tired and needed to drink water.
   ( )
   a. sleep   b. restart   c. lock

4. My computer doesn't allow me to type, which of these should I use?
   ( )
   a. restart   b. log off   c. lock

5. _____ and _____ are used to create an account. ( )
   a.   Name, username
   b.   Last-name, password
   c.   Username, password

6. UPS stands for _____. ( )
   a.   Uninterrupted Poverty Supply
   b.   Uninterrupted Power Super
   c.   Uninterrupted Power Supply

HCC - (QUICK-CHECK-3)

4

Date: _____

Match the start button functions to their meaning.

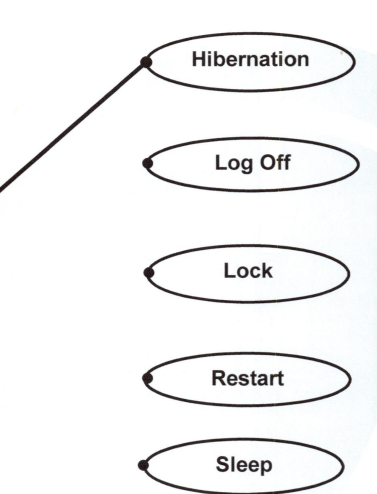

1. Desktop Lock, none can access your documents, browse your computer, or use programs on your computer.	Hibernation
2. It is shutting down a computer while keeping unsaved files and unclosed programs.	Log Off
3. It allows you to start up your computer when it fails.	Lock
4. It allows you to set the computer to auto-sleep to save on computer energy use.	Restart
5. Desktop log-off end all the process you are using in your profile account.	Sleep

INTRODUCTION TO COMPUTER - 2 (Explorer)

HCC - (QUICK-CHECK-4)

10

Date: _____

Use the given clues to complete the crossword puzzle below.

DOWN

3. _____ is used to rest when one is tired and needed to drink water

4. My computer doesn't allow me to type, which of these should I use?

ACROSS

1. _____ is used to go to another account on the screen.

2. _____ is used to sign out from an account.

5. _____ and _____ are used to create an account.

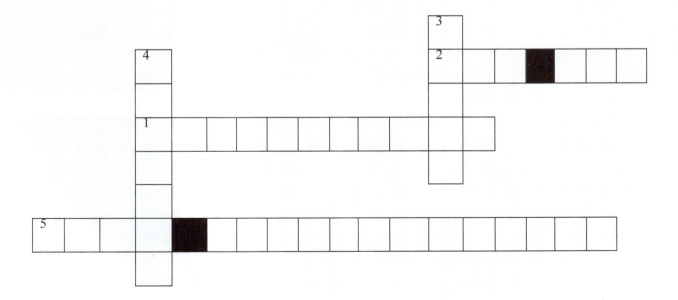

45

HCC - (QUICK-CHECK-5)

$\overline{4}$

Date: _____

Use the given clues to complete the crossword puzzle below.

DOWN

1. **Turn-on the UPS to _____ the flow of the current.**

2. **Turn-on the switch at the source of Power-_____.**

3. **Turn-on the Power-Switch of the _____.**

ACROSS

4. **Turn-on the _____ Unit.**

HCC - (QUICK-CHECK-6)

10

Date: _____

Tick (✓) *True* or *False* in each question provided below.

1. It is ok to let someone else use your computer user account if they are a friend of yours?

YES	
NO	

2. You can sit where ever you want in the computer lab?

YES	
NO	

3. It is ok to chew gum in the lab.

YES	
NO	

4. Students have to report any and all abuse of computer resources to the teacher.

YES	
NO	

5. Students can access the internet at any time while the class is in the lab.

YES	
NO	

6. A student can access any internet site if nobody but the student is looking at the screen.

YES	
NO	

7. Students can access their e-mail accounts from computers at school.

YES	
NO	

8. Students can access chat rooms at school.

YES	
NO	

9. Computers at School are mostly for fun, games, and entertainment.

YES	
NO	

10. The school district can find out where you have been and on what words you have been searching when using the Internet.

YES	
NO	

THE FUNCTIONS OF A COMPUTER SYSTEM

Lesson – 5.1: CAPABILITIES OF THE COMPUTER

1. We can type letters ABC and numbers 123 in the computer.

2. The computer can solve numbers 123 problems faster and simpler.

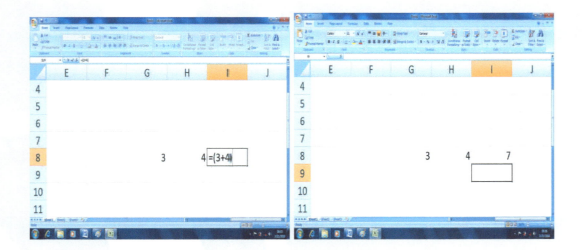

49

3.   We can draw and paint using the computer.

4.   The computer allows us to print colourful materials.

5.   The computer lets us play games.

Lesson – 5.2: USES OF THE COMPUTER

1. A computer tells cars when to **move** or **stop**.

2. Help us **talk** to our friends in far or near places.

2. It enables us to travel from one place to another **faster**.

3. It **checks** and **computes** our money in the bank.

4. Tells the weather **condition**.

FCS - (QUICK-CHECK-1)

10

Date: _____

Fill in the appropriate answer on each question.

1. We can _____ letters ABC and numbers 123 in the computer.

2. The computer can _____ numbers 1,2,3 problems faster and simpler.

3. We can _____ and _____ using the computer.

4. The computer allows us to _____ colourful materials.

5. Computer let us _____ game.

FCS - (QUICK-CHECK-2)

10

Date: _____

Fill in the appropriate answer on each question.

1. Computer _____ cars when to move or stop.

2. The computer is used to _____ to our friends in far or near places.

3. The computer makes travel from one place to another _____.

4. The computer is used to check and _____ our money in the bank.

5. Tell the _____ condition.

Chapter - 6

THE PORTS OF THE SYSTEM UNIT

All other hardware devices are connected to the computer through the back panel of the computer. Most of the ports and their connectors are colour-coded to aid the user in connecting the equipment properly.

LESSON – 6.1: WHAT IS A PORT?

a.)   A port is a connector or socket at the back of a computer.

b.)   An external device is plugged in there.

c.) Instruction and data are allowed to move between the computer and the device.

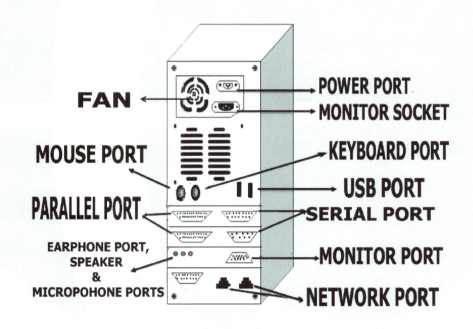

FAN
POWER PORT
MONITOR SOCKET
MOUSE PORT
KEYBOARD PORT
USB PORT
PARALLEL PORT
SERIAL PORT
EARPHONE PORT, SPEAKER & MICROPOHONE PORTS
MONITOR PORT
NETWORK PORT

LESSON – 6.2: Types of Port

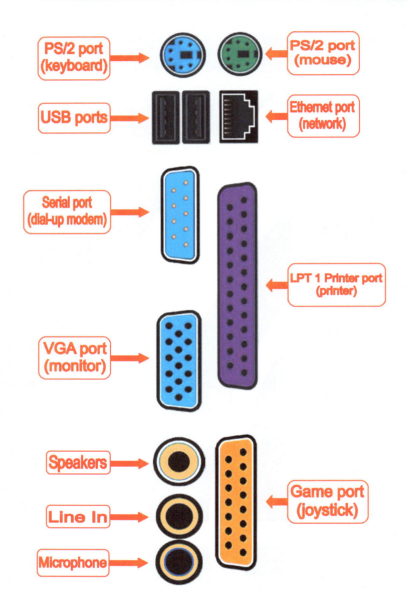

INTRODUCTION TO COMPUTER - 2 (Explorer)

S/N	TYPES OF SYSTEM UNIT PORTS
1.	KEYBOARD PORT
2.	PARALLEL PORT
3.	GAME PORT
4.	MONITOR PORT
5.	SPEAKER / MICROPHONE / EARPHONE PORTS
6.	UNIVERSAL SERIAL
7.	PORT (USB)
8.	MOUSE PORT
9.	SERIAL PORT
10.	ETHERNET PORT

1. KEYBOARD PORT: -

> A **keyboard** is connected to a **keyboard port**.

PS/2 port (keyboard)

2. PARALLEL PORT: -

➤ A port having **25 holes** is called parallel port.

➤ A **printer** or **tape** drive is connected to the system unit using this port.

➤ It is also known as a **male connecto**r.

3. GAME PORT: -

➤ A **joystick** is connected to a game port.

4. UNIVERSAL SERIAL BUS (USB).

- It is a new type of port that can connect up to 127 different peripheral devices with a single connector.

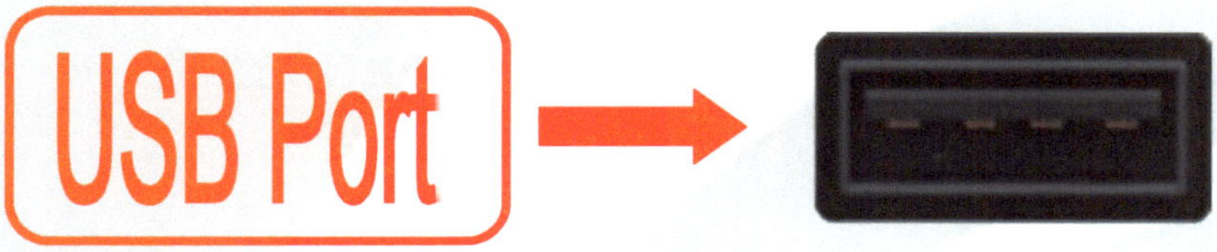

5. MONITOR PORT: -

- A **monitor** is connected to a monitor port.

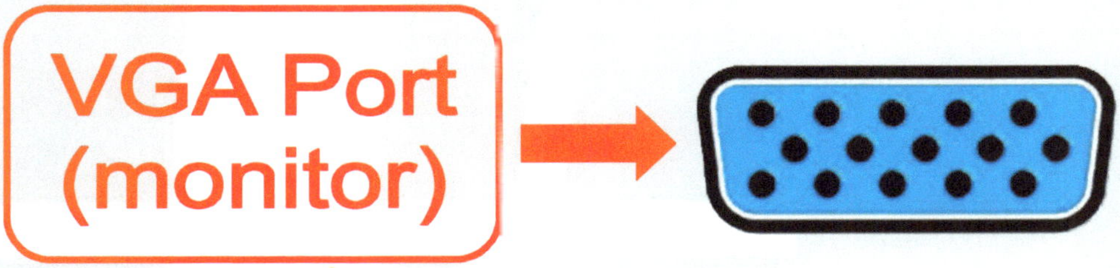

6. SERIAL PORT.

➢ A port having 9 or 25 pins is called a serial port.

➢ A **mouse**, **modem** or **scanner** is connected to the system unit using this port.

➢ It is also known as **female connector**.

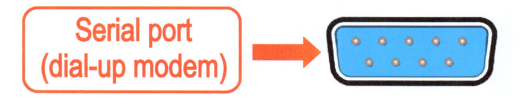

7. MOUSE PORT.

➢ The mouse is connected to mouse port.

8. ETHERNET PORT.

➤ Internet Cable is connected to the Ethernet port.

9. SPEAKER/MICROPHONE/ EARPHONE PORT.

➤ Speaker, Earphone and Microphone is connected to these three similar ports.

➤ One can identify them by the symbols or its colour.

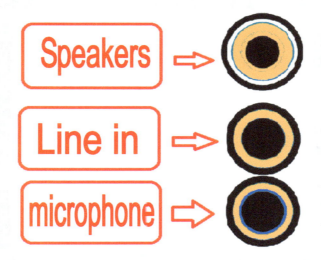

Fill in the blanks with the correct spelling

1. A ....(beyoakrd) is connected to a keyboard port.

2. A port having 25 holes is called .... (lleparal port).

3. A .... (terprin) or tape drive is connected to the System Unit using parallel port.

4. The parallel port is also known as a .... (lame) connector.

5. A joystick is connected to a ....(maeg) port.

6. Universal .... (rieSal) Bus is a new type of port that can connect up to 127 different peripheral devices with a single connector.

7. A .... (tornimo) is connected to a monitor port.

8. A port having 9 or 25 pins is called a .... (rialse) port.

9. A **mouse**, **modem** or .... (cansner) is connected to the system unit serial port.

10. The serial port is also known as female .... (torneccon).

INTRODUCTION TO COMPUTER - 2 (Explorer)

PSU - (QUICK-CHECK-2)

$\overline{6}$

Date: _____

LABEL THE PORTS OF THE SYSTEM UNIT

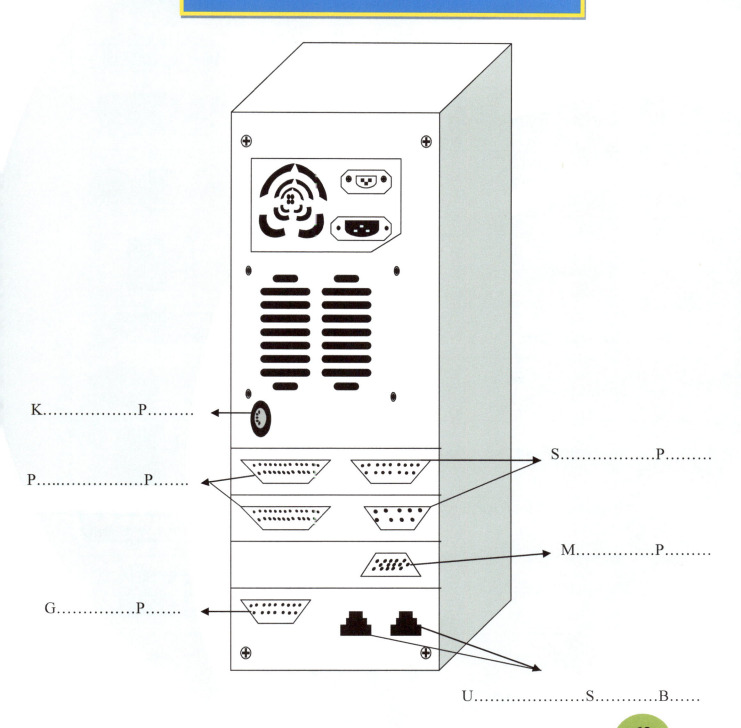

K.................P.........

P.....................P.......

S.................P.........

G..............P.......

M..............P.........

U.....................S...........B.....

63

PSU - (QUICK-CHECK-3)

$\dfrac{}{8}$

Date: _____

Match the ports of the system unit to their accurate names

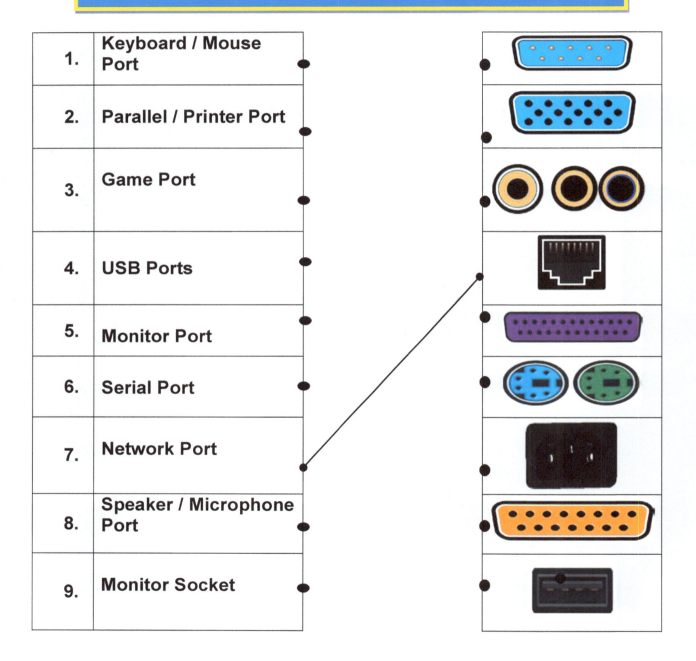

1.	Keyboard / Mouse Port	
2.	Parallel / Printer Port	
3.	Game Port	
4.	USB Ports	
5.	Monitor Port	
6.	Serial Port	
7.	Network Port	
8.	Speaker / Microphone Port	
9.	Monitor Socket	

Chapter - 7

USING THE COMPUTER KEYBOARD

LESSON – 7.1: THE MEANING OF THE KEYBOARD

What is a Keyboard?

❖ A keyboard is part of the computer that is used to type **letters**, **numbers** and **symbols** on your computer.

🏢 *Letters = A, B, C…… Z*

🏢 *Numbers = 1, 2, 3……, etc.*

🏢 *Symbols =!, @, #, $, %, etc.*

❖ The keyboard has some extra keys as well. It has 104,105, 107as the year goes; they more new keys were added.

❖ These keys are divided into seven different groups as shown below: -

Note: The keyboard has some extra keys as well. It has 104,105, 107 as the year goes, new more keys were added.

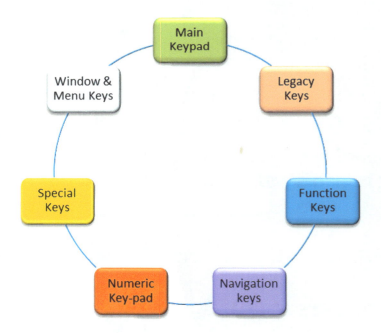

INTRODUCTION TO COMPUTER - 2 (Explorer)

LESSON – 7.2: PARTS AND LAYOUT OF THE KEYBOARD

🖎 Whether you're writing a letter or entering numerical data, your keyboard is the main way to enter information into your computer.

🖎 But do you know that you can also use your keyboard to control your computer?

🖎 Learning just a few simple keyboard commands (instructions to your computer) can help you work more efficiently.

🖎 This lesson covers the basics of keyboard operation and gets you started with keyboard commands.

The keys on your keyboard are divided into seven groups based on their functions:

1. MAIN KEYPAD *(Alphabet Keys):*

- ✍ These keys have 26 letters of the English alphabet marked on them in capital letters.

- ✍ NOTE: Punctuation marks like comma, full-stop, question mark, etc., also form a part of the **main keypad**.

- ✍ Also, the tab, caps-lock key, enter key and backspace key are part of this group of keys.

2. FUNCTION KEYS:

- ✍ These keys are there on top of the keyboard above the number keys.

- ✍ They are marked: F1, F2, F3, ... F12.

- ✍ Each of these keys is used for special jobs.

INTRODUCTION TO COMPUTER - 2 (Explorer)

3. NAVIGATION KEYS:

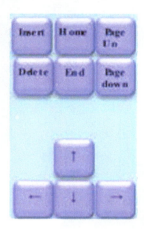

✍ They are used to move the cursor around the screen.

✍ To move the cursor to where we want it to be.

✍ Move the selected text/object to the desired place on the monitor.

✍ Above these keys are a block of six keys that include

📖 **Insert** key which allows text to be inserted.

📖 **Delete** key which erase text on the right side of the cursor.

📖 **Home key** is often used to return the user to the beginning of the line.

📖 **End key** which move cursor to the end line of a document.

69

4. NUMERIC KEY-PAD:

✌ This is the second set of number keys on the keyboard of a computer.

✌ The numeric keypad is used to do mathematical data on the monitor.

✌ Example: multiplication sign *, subtraction sign -, division sign /, addition sign +, and decimal sign .. It also has enter key etc.

5. WINDOWS AND MENU KEY:

✌ The **window key** opens the start menu of windows operating system. While, the **menu key** opens a pop-up menu such as Ms-word, Desktop screen, etc.

6. SPECIAL KEYS:

- 👌 These keys do special jobs as the function keys does.

- 👌 But there is a difference between the jobs of the two.

- 👌 In the case of the **function keys**, the **job assigned** to it **may change**.

- 👌 But each **special key** is used for a **job** which **never changes**.

7. LEGACY KEYS:

- 👌 Legacy Keys are similar as special keys. The difference between both is that Legacy keys can do specific function without depressing the key and another key simultaneously.

- 👌 Esc normally used to interrupt or cancel an activity.

- 👌 Print screen key take an image of the current screen to the computer clipboard.

- 👌 The Scroll lock key as the name implies, depressing the key will temporarily stop the scrolling of text in a window.

✍ Pause/Break key, depressing this key will automatically pause a text-mode from operating.

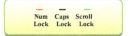

✍ It is used to know when Number Lock, Caps Lock or Scroll Lock is ON or OFF.

LESSON – 7.3: FINGERS PLACEMENT

1. Fingers placed on home row (ASDF JKL;)

   ✎ Fingers curved in a scratch-like position and the thumb positioned close to the center of the space bar.

   ✎ Palms, wrists, lower arms parallel to the slant of the keyboard

Left		Right	
1. Pinky		1. Pinky	
2. Ring		2. Ring	
3. Middle		3. Middle	
4. Pointer		4. Pointer	
5. Thumb		5. Thumb	

2. Proper Finger placement in the keyboard

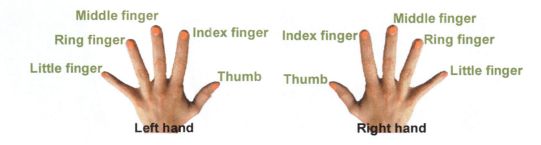

✍ Little finger Left: It is used to depress: - Z A Q   Shift Caps-lock   Tab ` 1   (keys)

✍ Ring finger left: It is used to depress: - X   S   W   2 (keys)

✍ Middle finger left: It is used to depress: C   D   E   3 (keys)

✍ Index finger left: It is used to depress: V   B   F   G   R   T   4   5 (keys)

✍ Thumb left: It is used to depress: Spacebar key

✍ Thumb right: It is used to depress: Spacebar key

✍ Index finger right: It is used to depress: N   M   H   J   Y   U   6   7 (keys)

✍ Middle finger right: It is used to depress: ,   K   I   8 (keys)

✍ Ring finger right: It is used to depress: - .   L   O   9 (keys)

✍ Little finger right: It is used to depress: - arrows keys /   shift   ;   , enter   P   [   ]   \   0   -   = Backspace

- We shall learn about the *special keys* on the keyboard of a computer. Special key is used for a job which never changes.

- One thing more, the special keys are not there together at a place on the keyboard. The number of the special keys is about 30. But here in this lesson, we shall study about only a few basic ones out of them.

BASIC PC SHORTCUT KEYS

 It is highly recommended that all users keep a good reference of the below shortcut keys and/or try to memorize the below keys. Doing so will dramatically increase your productivity.

Control Key

∞ Control Key **Ctrl** Depressing the Ctrl key while clicking allows multiple selections.

∞ Holding the Ctrl key down and pressing other key combinations will initiate quite a few actions. Some of the more common ones are listed below.

1. **Ctrl** + **A** Select **All** items

2. **Ctrl** + **B** Add or remove **Bold** formatting

3. **Ctrl** + **C** **Copy**, places the **selected/highlighted** copy on the clipboard.

4. **Ctrl** + **D** **Open** font dialog box.

5. **Ctrl** + **E** **Centre** alignment.

6. **Ctrl** + **F** Opens the **Find what:** dialog box.

7. **Ctrl** + **G** **Go** to a particular **page** in a document.

8. **Ctrl** + **H** **Replace**, brings up the **Find and Replace** dialog box.

9. **Ctrl** + **I** Add or remove **Italic** formatting.

10. **Ctrl** + **J** to **justify** text full.

11. **Ctrl** + **K** to **hyperlink** selected text.

12. **Ctrl** + **L** to **justify** text left.

13. **Ctrl** + **M** to **increase** Indent.

14. **Ctrl** + **N** Window, In Internet Explorer, opens a **New Window**.

15. **Ctrl** + **O** **Open**, brings up a browse dialog box and allows you to select a file to open.

16. **Ctrl** + **P** **Print,** brings up a print dialog box and allows you to set your printing style.

17. **Ctrl** + **Q** **Remove** Paragraph formats.

18. **Ctrl** + **R** **Justify** text **Right**.

19. **Ctrl** + **S** **Save,** brings up a save as dialog box and allows you to save your work using your name.

20. **Ctrl** + **T** **Increase** Hanging Indent.

21. **Ctrl** + **U** Add or remove **Underline** formatting.

22. **Ctrl** + **V** **Paste**, inserts the copy on the clipboard into the area where your flashing cursor I is positioned or the area you have <mark>selected/highlighted</mark>.

23. **Ctrl** + **W** **Close** will close the document currently open.

24. **Ctrl** + **X** **Cut**, removes the <mark>selected/highlighted</mark> copy and places it on the clipboard.

25. **Ctrl** + **Y** **Redo** last command.

26. **Ctrl** + **Z** **Undo** last command or displays the last work.

27. **Ctrl** + **Esc** Open the Start menu (or use the Windows Key if you have one).

28. **Ctrl** + **=** Spell checker.

29. **Ctrl** + **Shift** **While** dragging a file to create a shortcut.

30. **Ctrl** + **Tab** Allows movement (toggle) from one open window to the next in an application with more than one open window.

Other keys

ALT Depressing the ALT key with another key will initiate various actions.

Space Bar Create a space between words.

Enter Creates a new **Paragraph** <p> (¶).

Backspace While working with text, use this key to delete characters to the left side of the cursor.

Delete While working with text, use this key to delete characters to the right side of the cursor. This key can also be used to delete selected files.

Up Arrow Navigate in a document to the line above.

Right Arrow Navigate in a document one character to the right.

31. **Down Arrow** Navigate in a document to the line below. Hold the Ctrl key down as you press this key to move to the beginning of the second line below.

32. **Left Arrow** Navigate in a document one character to the left. Hold the Ctrl key down as you press this key to move one word to the left.

79

UCK - (QUICK-CHECK-1)

Date: _____

| Fill in the parenthesis with the correct answer | 21 |

1. What keys do you use to move the cursor around your text?   (   )
    A. Enter   B. Arrow keys   C. Ctrl shift

2. What keys do you use the select or highlight part of the text?   (   )
    A. Arrow keys   B. Enter   C. Shift + arrow keys

3. What keys do you use to make the text bold?   (   )
    A. Ctrl + B   B. Ctrl + D   C. Shift + B

4. What keys do you use to copy something?   (   )
    A. Ctrl + X   B. Ctrl + Z   C. Ctrl + C

5. What keys do you use to cut text or pictures?   (   )
    A. Ctrl + X   B. Ctrl + C   C. Ctrl + Z

6. What keys do you use to paste?   (   )
    A. Ctrl + P   B. Ctrl +X   C. Ctrl + V

7. What keys do you use to underline the text?   (   )
    A. Ctrl + X   B. Ctrl + U   C. Ctrl + Z

8. What keys do you use to undo the last thing you did?   (   )
    A. Ctrl + U   B. Ctrl + L   C. Ctrl + Z

9. What keys do you use to redo the last action?   (   )
    A. Ctrl + R   B. Ctrl + D   C. Ctrl + Y

10. What keys do you use to open a new document?   (   )
    A. Ctrl + N   B. Shift + N   C. Alt + N

11. What keys do you use to select all?   (   )
    A. Ctrl + S   B. Ctrl + A   C. Shift + A

12. What keys do you use to save?   (   )
   A. Ctrl + S   B. Shift + F12   C. Alt + F12

13. The icons you see on your desktop represent.   (   )

   A.   Programs, data files and Recycle bin.
   B.   Only data files
   C.   Only devices attached to your computer
   D.   Only programs

14. Which button do you click on, to begin the process of shutting down a PC? (   )
   A.   The My Computer icon
   B.   The Start button
   C.   The Taskbar
   D.   The Control Panel button

15. Which should I save my school homework?   (   )
   a. Drive D: b. Drive C: c. Drive None:

16. _____ key is used to type the symbols on top of a key or change a
   small letter to a capital letter.   (   )
   a. Caplock   b. Shift   c. Delete

17. _____ key is used to make a space between words during typing.
                                                                                     (   )
   a. Backspace   b. Space-bar   c. Shift

18. _____ key is used to change the letter to a capital or small letter.
                                                                                     (   )
   a. Caplock   b. Shift   c. Delete

19. _____ key is used to erase any character before the cursor's current
   position (to the left).   (   )
   a. Spacebar   b. Backspace   c. Caplock

20. _____ key is used to erase any character after the cursor's current
   position (to the right).   (   )
   a. Caplock   b. Delete   c. Shift

21. If I want to move from line **ten** to line **one** in a passage on my computer screen,
   which of the keys should I press? _____.   (   )

   a. Arrow keys   b. Backspace key   c. jump key

81

UCK - (QUICK-CHECK-2)

Date: _____

Section-A

‾‾
10

> **Fill in the blank with the correct result.**

What should be the result of the following if you press _____;
(Note this symbol is the cursor (|).

1. **DELETE-KEY**: Flower girl has se|ven oranges in her bag.

   Ans: _____

2. **CAPLOCK-KEY**: I like teacher Douglas.

   Ans: _____

3. **BACKSPACE**: Monkey likes to eat | banana.

   Ans: _____

4. **SPACEBAR**: Mr. James pro|mise to take our class to the Zoo.

   Ans: _____

5. **SPACEBAR**: Elep|hant kingdom.

   Ans: _____

Section-B

10

Correct the following sentences.

1. Anytime teacher announces P.E day, my class alWays shout for joy.

   Correction:

   _____

   _____

2. Our monthly test is today; i know i will not have less than 90% in My computer test.

   Correction:

   _____

   _____

Homework-1

Use the given clues to complete the crossword puzzle below.

DOWN

1. Avoid exposing your computer to _____.
3. Do not _____ the computer around.
6. Always tidy up the computer _____.
7. Do not take _____ or _____ to the computer room.
8. Always plug your computer to an Uninterrupted Power _____ (UPS).
10. _____ down your computer properly.

ACROSS

2. Do not use magnetic object near the _____.
4. Take off your _____ before you enter the computer room.
5. Shut the _____ of the computer room properly.
9. _____ the computer when a brownout occurs.

Homework-2   Date: _____

Choose the options in parenthesis to fill-in the blank spaces.

1. The computer is an electronic machine that _____, process, _____ and stores data.   (   )

   a. output, output   b. output, input   c. process, input

2. _____ is a plate that stores information.   (   )

   a. Computer   b. Output   c. Disk   d. Storage

3. Computer accept data when we type.   (   )

   a. Input   b. Output   c. Process d. Storage

4. Computer check what we type on the keyboard.   (   )

   a. Input   b. Output   c. Process d. Storage

5. Computer displays what we type on the monitor.   (   )

   a. Input   b. Output   c. Process d. Storage

6. The computer saves our work on computer memory.   (   )

   a. Input   b. Output   c. Process d. Storage

85

Choose the options in parenthesis to fill-in the blank spaces.

1) What type of device is a computer monitor?   (   )

a) Input   b) Output   c) Software   d) Storage

2) What type of device is a computer keyboard?   (   )

a) Input   b) Output   c) Software   d) Storage

3) What type of devices are computer speakers or headphones? (   )

a) Input   b) Output   c) Software   d) Storage

4) What type of device is a computer printer?   (   )

a) Input   b) Output   c) Software   d) Storage

5) What type of device is a computer mouse?   (   )

a) Input   b) Output   c) Software   d) Storage

References:

▤ Er. Swati Raghuvanshi, Tuesday, 1 January 2013. Computer and its components. [Online], Available: http://er-swati-raghuvanshi.blogspot.com/2013/01/compuer-and-its-components.html [Accessed 23 August 2013]

▤ (No Name) (No date) What are computers? [Online]. Available: http://wikieducator.org/User:Tzaynah/TComputingCourse [Accessed 10 August 2013]

▤ Martin's, (No date), Applied Unit 4 - ict solutions [Online]. Available: http://www.kgv.ac.uk/intranet/it/maf/applied_unit_4/Hardware/ports_connectors/ports_connectors.php [Accessed 10 August 2013]

▤ Jo Black, 7-30-03. *Basic Computer Knowledge Quiz* [Online]. Available: http://www.joblack59.com/computers/quiz_01/popquiz.htm [Accessed 10 August 2013]

▤ (No Name) (No date) *Computer keyboard shortcut keys* [Online]. Available: http://www.iswhat.org/whatis/shortcut.html [Accessed 10 August 2013]

▤ Computer Hope, (No date), When was the first computer invented? [Online]. Available: http://www.computerhope.com/issues/ch000984.htm [Accessed 23 August 2013]

www.ingramcontent.com/pod-product-compliance
Lightning Source LLC
Chambersburg PA
CBHW041420050326

40689CB00002B/588